Maximus

The Brave

Teri Francis & Vanessa Keen

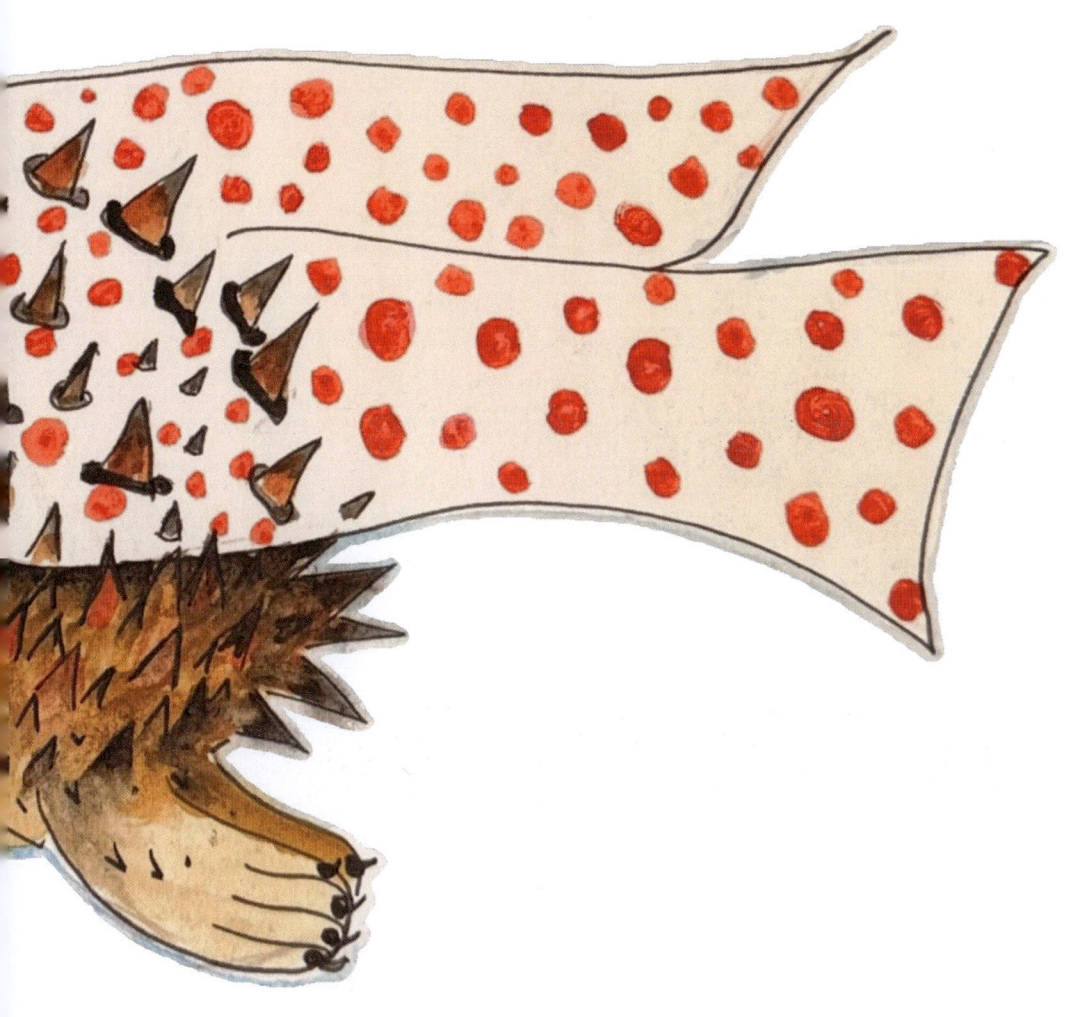

Dedication from Teri

For my wonderful grandchildren Madison, Marley, Memphis and Hudson who shine a light on our lives. With love, Nana xx

Dedication from Vanessa

For Florence, Madeleine, and Poppy, your loving, bright imagination always inspires endless fun, laughter and creative adventures. With love, Nana xxx

Copyright © 2025 Authors Teri Francis and Vanessa Keen.

All rights reserved.

No part of this book may be reproduced, stored in a retrieval system, or transmitted in any form or by any means—electronic, mechanical, photocopying, recording, or otherwise—without the prior written permission of the authors, except for brief quotations in reviews or scholarly works.

Published by Arkedia Publishers, 2025.

Maximus is a tiny hedgehog who sometimes feels sad and lonely because the other animals in the wood seem bigger, braver, and stronger than him.

Nutty is a playful grey squirrel who loves to surprise her friends with her cheeky tricks!

Nutty's best game is to shoot nuts at the animals passing by with her incredible nutapault.

Nutty especially loves to surprise Maximus, who squeals with fright. He will scurry under a huge pile of leaves that stick to his prickles, making him look like a funny, shaking bush.

One day, Nutty watched as Maximus sat on a comfy log, carefully laying out his favourite red spotted napkin upon his lap.

Just as he was about to take a bite out of his huge, delicious biscuit, Nutty leapt out of the tree, letting out a big, playful giggle as she jumped.

Nutty landed with an enormous ....

THUD

And.........

WHOOSH

Maximus whizzed into the air, still clutching his biscuit and with his napkin waving around him like a superhero's cloak.

With a loud **TWANG**, Maximus found himself stuck to the tree by his prickles, and his little napkin flopped right over his eyes!

Poor Maximus, he couldn't see anything except the red spots on his napkin.

He was so very scared!

"EEEK HELP HELP!"

He squealed.

Nutty held her tummy, rolling around laughing uncontrollably at the silly sight,

(Maximus, his legs flapping furiously beneath his napkin).

She was laughing so loudly she didn't hear Peat, an enormous black badger, thundering towards her.

Peat was shaking his head, his body spinning, as his legs ran faster and faster, then zigzagging as he got closer and closer until. **BOOM!**

Peat crashed into Nutty, who somersaulted several times before smashing into the apple tree (where, unfortunately, Maximus was still stuck).

*Nutty went to stand up, but **Plop**, an apple, fell onto her head, quickly followed by another. She sat down, the world was spinning, and she felt very dizzy.*

Peat was still running in circles, grunting, and howling, making the most awful noise. "**ARGGHH OOORRR**"

Then, with a very loud crack and snap, Maximus dropped down from the tree and landed splat right on Peat's back.

Peat reared up on his back legs, shaking his body from side to side like a wild horse.

"ARRGH"

Maximus tried his best not to fall, holding on tight to Peat's ears.

"**WOAH,**" screamed Maximus, "**STOP STOP!**"

Shouting didn't seem to work, so he said more softly "**Shhh**, it's ok, it's ok, calm your beans, please stop moving, if you stop, I can get off."

Peat slowed down just enough for Maximus to slide off.

"Phew!" Said Maximus as he scurried quickly towards Nutty (who was still dazed from the collision with Peat, and the apples!)

Maximus and Nutty peeped out from the bushes to see what was happening and saw Peat sitting on the ground, exhausted.

He was still snorting and grunting, but he was much quieter now.

Maximus was still feeling a bit nervous, but he stood up, snuffled around, and took a few small steps towards Peat.

"Oh, my goodness, what on earth is stuck on your nose?" It was a big, red, shiny can and it was stuck tight!

Maximus puffed himself up and took a deep breath. He took a few more cautious steps toward Peat.

"Um, hello, I'm Maximus. Do you need some help?"

Peat looked up, surprised. He shook his body fiercely, **"ARGhhh!"** *Maximus was worried, but then he could see Peat wasn't angry. He was just very, very scared.*

Maximus bravely edged closer. He could see he clearly needed help.

Placing his tiny paws on either side of the can, he pulled, and pulled and tugged, and tugged, huffing and puffing, but the can would not budge.

"Nutty", called Maximus, "Come and hold onto my legs, and when I say pull, pull as hard as you can". Nutty cautiously crept up to Maximus and held his legs as tight as he could.

"Ok, now pull!" He shouted.

They were pulling and tugging, huffing and puffing like crazy. Then, with a loud **pop** and a very satisfying **boing,** the can was off!

They pulled so hard they tumbled backwards, unable to stop themselves falling, crashing into a big heap of twigs and leaves.

Nutty landed on Maximus's back (which was very prickly!), and the can was now balanced nicely on top of Nutty's head, like a very big shiny crown!

Peat looked at them both and let out a soft chuckle, which grew louder and louder. His body was shaking with his laughter.

Oh dear!
With all the shaking, another apple dropped from the tree and fell right onto poor Peats' head.

All three sat in silence for a moment, unsure of what was coming next.

Then Nutty let out a muffled giggle, which was closely followed by Maximus and then Peat.

Their laughter got louder and louder, and the more they laughed, the more the apples fell.

Today had been quite an adventure.
"You were so brave, Maximus!" said Nutty.
"And kind too!" Peat added.
"And who knew hedgehogs could fly?"
Nutty said.
"Thanks to my spotty superhero napkin,"
Maximus chuckled.

"Group hedgehug?" Maximus asked.
"Sure, we can," said Nutty.
"Oh, please don't say can," snorted Peat.

And after one big hedgehug, the three friends began to make their way safely home.

Some Prickly Facts

- *Hedgehogs are lactose intolerant, so they shouldn't have milk to drink.*

- *Although hedgehogs have poor eyesight, they have excellent hearing, a super sense of smell and curved claws to help them dig for food.*

- *Hedgehogs live 8 - 10 years and have a litter of 4 - 6 hoglets.*

- *Hedgehogs are gardeners' best friends because they will eat the slugs and snails.*

- *Hedgehogs prefer the night; they can swim, climb, and move very fast.*

Some Prickly Questions

 *What are baby hedgehogs called?*

 *Why are hedgehogs' claws curved?*

 *Who is a hedgehog's best friend?*

 *What should hedgehogs not drink?*

 *What are hedgehogs good at?*

Brave
Being brave means trying to do the right thing, even when it feels hard or a little scary.

Brave

Kind
Kindness means being nice and helping others when

Kind

Printed in Dunstable, United Kingdom